Women
and the U. S.
Constitution,
1776–1920

Other Titles in this Series:

The War Power: Original and Contemporary
by **Louis Fisher**

Women and the U.S. Constitution, 1776–1920

by **Jean H. Baker**

**Published by the
American Historical Association
400 A Street, SE
Washington, D.C. 20003
www.historians.org**

JEAN H. BAKER is a professor of history at Goucher College. She is the author of several books, including *Sisters: The Lives of America's Suffragists*; *Mary Todd Lincoln: A Biography*; and *Affairs of Party: The Political Culture of Northern Democrats in Mid-Nineteenth Century America*, and editor of *Votes for Women: The Struggle for Suffrage Revisited*.

AHA EDITORS: Robert B. Townsend, Liz Townsend

LAYOUT: Chris Hale

© 2009 by the American Historical Association
ISBN: 978-0-87229-163-8

Published in 2009 by the American Historical Association. As publisher, the American Historical Association does not adopt official views on any field of history and does not necessarily agree or disagree with the views expressed in this book.

Library of Congress Cataloging-in-Publication Data

Baker, Jean H.

Women and the U.S. Constitution, 1776-1920 / by Jean H. Baker

p. cm.—(New essays in American constitutional history)

Includes bibliographical references.

ISBN 978-0-87229-163-8 (alk. paper)

1. Women--Legal status, laws, etc.--United States--History. 2. Women's rights--United States--History. 3. Married women--Legal status, laws, etc.--United States--History. 4. Women--United States--Suffrage--History. I. Title.

KF478.B35 2008

342.7308'78--dc22   2008044691

Table of Contents

Series Introduction

*N*ew Essays on American Constitutional History is published by the American Historical Association, in association with the Institute for Constitutional Studies. This series follows the lead of its predecessor, the Bicentennial Essays on the Constitution, published by the AHA under the editorship of Herman Belz as part of the commemoration of the two hundredth anniversary of the Constitution over two decades ago. The goal remains the same. The essays are intended to provide both students and teachers with brief, accessible, and reliable introductions to some of the most important aspects of American constitutional development. The essays reflect the leading scholarship in the field and address topics that are classic, timely, and always important.

American constitutionalism is characterized by a series of tensions. Such tensions are persistent features of American constitutional history, and they make a frequent appearance in these essays. The American tradition emphasizes the importance of written constitutions. The United States Constitution declares that "this Constitution" is the "supreme law of the land." But time moves on. Politics and society are ever changing. How do we manage the tension between being faithful to a written constitutional text and adapting to changing political circumstances? To the extent that the American brand of constitutionalism binds us to the past, creates stability, and slows political change, how do we balance these conservative forces with the pressures of the moment that might demand departures from inherited ways of doing things and old ideas about rights and values? We sometimes change the terms of the old text through amendment or wholesale replacement of one constitution with another (from the Articles of Confederation to the Constitution at the national level, or more often at the state level), but we apply and adapt the inherited constitutional text through interpretation and practice. All the while, we manage the tension between being faithful to the text that we have and embracing the "living constitution" that grows out of that text.

Law figures prominently in the American constitutional tradition. Our written constitutions are understood to be fundamental laws and part of our legal code. They are the foundation of our legal system and superior to all other laws. They provide legally enforceable rules for judges and others to follow. Judges and lawyers play an important role in interpreting American constitutions and translating the bare bones of the original text into the detailed body of doctrine known as constitutional law. It has often been the dream of judges, lawyers, and legal scholars to insulate constitutional law from the world of politics. There is a long-held aspiration for judges and lawyers to be able to spin out constitutional law in accord with established principles of justice, reason, and tradition. But politics has also been central to the history of American constitutionalism. Constitutions are created by political actors and serve political purposes. Once in place, constitutional rules and values are politically contested, and they are interpreted and put into practice by politicians and political activists, as well as by judges. The tension between law and politics is a persistent one in American constitutional history.

A final tension of note has been between power and liberty. In the modern tradition, constitutional government is limited government. Constitutions impose limits and create mechanisms for making those constraints effective. They specify what the boundaries of government power are and what rights individuals and groups have against government. But there is also an older tradition, in which constitutions organize and empower government. The U.S. Constitution contains both elements. Many of its provisions, especially the amendments, limit government. These are some of the most celebrated features of the Constitution, and they have become the basis for much of the constitutional law that has been developed by the judiciary. But the Constitution was specifically adopted to empower the federal government and create new, better institutions that could accomplish national objectives. Both the U.S. Constitution and the state constitutions are designed to gather and direct government power to advance the public good. Throughout American constitutional history, judges, politicians, and activists have struggled over the proper balance between empowering government and limiting government and over the best understanding of the rights of individuals and the public welfare.

These essays examine American constitutionalism, not a particular constitutional text. The U.S. Constitution figures prominently in these essays, as it does in American history, but the American constitutional tradition includes other foundational documents, including notably the state constitutions. These texts are a guide to the subject matter of these essays, but they are not exhaustive of it. Laws, court decisions, administrative actions, and custom, along with founding documents, perform constitutional functions in the American political system, just as they do in the British system where there is no single written "constitution." Whether "written" or "unwritten," constitutions perform certain common tasks. Constitutions define the organic structures of government, specifying the basic institutions for making and implementing public policy, including the processes for altering the constitution itself. Constitutions distribute powers among those institutions of government, delegating, enumerating, prohibiting, and reserving powers to each governmental body. The flip side of entrusting power and discretion to governmental bodies is the definition of limits on those powers, the specification of individual and collective rights. Constitutions also specify who participates in the institutions of government and how and to whom the power of government applies. That is, constitutions identify the structures of citizenship and political jurisdiction. Across its seven articles and twenty-seven amendments, the U.S. Constitution addresses all of these topics, but the text is only a starting point. These topics form the subject matter of New Essays on American Constitutional History.

Writing early in the twentieth century, the great constitutional historian Edward Corwin observed that relatively few citizens actually read the U.S. Constitution, despite its brevity. He thought that this was in part because the "real constitution of the United States has come to mean something very different from the document" itself. The document laid out the framework of government, but "the real scope of the powers which it should exercise and of the rights which it should guarantee was left, to a very great extent, for future developments to determine." Understanding American constitutionalism requires understanding American constitutional history. It is a history of contestation and change, creation and elaboration. These essays aim to illuminate that history.

—*Keith E. Whittington,*
Princeton University

—*Gerry Leonard,*
Boston University School of Law

Introduction

As the fundamental national charter of governance for the inhabitants of the United States—whether native or foreign-born, male or female, black or white—the Constitution of the United States, along with its 27 amendments, defines the opportunities, rights, privileges, and obligations of its population. Intended as a structure of government for a new, experimental republic based on the sovereignty of the people, the arrangements made in Philadelphia in 1787 nevertheless reached well beyond formal organization to affect the everyday lives of Americans. This connection to the people, sometimes obscured by formal organizational procedures separating the executive, legislative, and judicial powers as well as state and national authority, became more obvious with the addition of the ten amendments comprising the Bill of Rights. In these amendments, the protection of various rights shielded individuals from the national government. In both the Bill of Rights and the United States Constitution, however, gender remained an invisible category. The framers were men who, while cognizant of economics and politics, overlooked what by the middle of the twentieth century would emerge as significant matters of female equality with relevance to constitutional, not just statutory or common, law. The authors of the Constitution never envisioned any explicit consideration of women as part of "We the People."

Thus American women had only a peripheral, contested constitutional history before the ratification of the women's suffrage amendment in 1920. They played no role in the authorship of either the original 1787 document or the Bill of Rights, and they were largely excluded from the Constitution's application. Yet the possibilities for a constitutional history for women began after the Civil War with optimistic expectations that the Reconstruction Amendments—especially the Fourteenth and Fifteenth—would eliminate the disenfranchisement of women. But the courts continued to base their judgments on traditional views of women's place in the family.

In time, understandings of democracy, representative government, and the consent of the governed—all venerated American ideals inherited from its revolutionary beginnings—broadened. As a result, and especially after the ratification of the Fourteenth and Fifteenth Amendments, a movement toward equality for freed slaves and women occurred. There were several forms of access to the Constitution in this slow process, as women employed state and federal courts to contest their legal disabilities, especially the prohibitions against their voting.

The women's rights movement began in earnest in the middle of the nineteenth century when activist women sought constitutional inclusion as individual rights-bearing Americans. In 1848, the women at Seneca Falls, in their Declaration of Sentiments, based their claims on the natural rights of humanity, first enunciated in the 1776 Declaration of Independence. Specifically, they argued that the "unalienable right to life, liberty, and the pursuit of happiness" included the right for women to vote, to serve on juries, to control their own property, and, among other resolutions, to work in the professions and to be educated in institutions of higher learning that barred admission on the basis of their sex.

As the nineteenth century progressed, reformers sought to change public opinion, referring to themselves in common sense terms as part of "We the People." After the ratification of the Fourteenth Amendment in 1868, with its pledge that "all persons born or naturalized in the United States … are citizens of the United States," they properly categorized themselves as citizens of the republic and, as such, voters and political actors who could serve as jurors and officeholders. The slow contested march began with efforts to change the denial of married women's property rights. Later, challenges in court cases brought under the articles of the Fourteenth Amendment reached the Supreme Court and became the focus of the struggle for women's civil rights. Still, progress was slow, and even today, after the failure of the Equal Rights Amendment in the 1980s, there is no constitutional provision that prohibits discrimination against women. Moreover, federal and state laws involving women are not subjected to the same judicial strict scrutiny as those involving race.

By the end of the nineteenth century, women, now organized into national suffrage organizations, concentrated on the vote. Several court cases testified to this struggle for federal civil rights under the U.S. Constitution. In two cases decided by the Supreme Court during Reconstruction, women sought inclusion in the national electorate through their status as citizens, arguing that they were denied their constitutionally protected "privileges and immunities" under the first section of the Fourteenth Amendment. The Supreme Court rejected this claim in *Minor v. Happersett* (1874). Claiming citizenship under the first article of the Fourteenth Amendment and with citizenship the right to vote, Virginia Minor was denied the right to vote in the presidential election of 1872. In the subsequent court case, one of the first reviewed by the U.S. Supreme Court affecting women, the registrar's action was upheld. In a constricted reading of the Fourteenth Amendment's privileges and immunities clause, the Court ruled that the right to vote was not a necessary privilege of citizenship guaranteed to all persons born or naturalized in the United States. In practice, such a restrictive interpretation was specifically aimed at women.

In the case of *Bradwell v. Illinois* (1873), married women were denied the right to practice law on the grounds that the opportunity to enter the legal profession pertained only to state citizenship. *Bradwell* was as philosophically devastating a legal decision for women as the notorious *Dred Scott* decision of 1857 was for blacks. Shortly after the Court refused in the Slaughterhouse Cases to interpret the Fourteenth Amendment as expanding federal power very far, even with respect to race, the *Bradwell* Court refused to extend federal authority in favor of women's citizenship rights. It deferred to traditional state prerogatives and rejected a federal right of access to the professions for women. The Court's sentiment, moreover, was shared by many federal lawmakers. In the debates over the Fourteenth Amendment, congressmen and senators frequently expressed their fears that states' rights would disappear or, as Senator Hendricks of Indiana warned, "be done away with."[1]

The extension of suffrage as a right of federal citizenship was denied on the same basis as the denial of equal opportunity to practice a profession: women were not legally autonomous. And in dicta that today is quoted to demonstrate the endurance of the patriarchal common law's influence on constitutional interpretation, "the paramount destiny and mission of woman," wrote Justice Bradley in *Bradwell*, "are to fulfill the noble and benign offices of wife and mother."[2] Hence the state of Illinois had every right to bar Myra Bradwell from admission to its bar.

By the twentieth century, women's reform efforts concentrated almost entirely on obtaining the vote—the essential access card for inclusion in the body politic. Earlier this struggle had focused on efforts to change the gendered voting requirements at the state level, but by 1910 most groups rallied around a national women's suffrage amendment. After the *Minor* and *Bradwell* decisions by the Supreme Court, there could be no change for women unless their political nullity was ended constitutionally. This could only be accomplished for all American women by an amendment to the U.S. Constitution.

The common law seemed increasingly archaic in the modernizing society of the early twentieth century. Yet women had to obtain their rights from reluctant male legislators and judges who were generally uninterested in giving up their domestic authority and who remained saturated with paternalistic beliefs that women neither needed nor wanted the vote and should stay at home. Inclusion came slowly and grudgingly. Finally, the Nineteenth Amendment was passed by two-thirds of Congress and in 1920 was ratified by three-quarters of the states. Women took their place as equals in the electorate, as the amendment began an explicit process of ending women's peripheral contact with their nation's constitution. Gradually, constitutional principles, especially from the due process and equal protection phrases of the Fourteenth Amendment, were applied to government action in matters involving sex, but from 1776–1920, the equalization of opportunities, rights, and privileges for women was not considered a judicial function.

1

The Common Law of Domestic Relations

he civic invisibility of women did not arrive with the American Revolution and the subsequent writing of the U.S. Constitution. Rather, the common law was among Britain's early seventeenth-century exports to its subjects in the colonies, and, especially in the area of domestic relations (for it also covered property rights, treason, and other matters), the common law was widely believed to incorporate "the applied customs of the community." As early as 1630, John Winthrop, the governor of Massachusetts, gave a ringing endorsement of the common law and its effect on women once they had married: "... he is her lord, and she is to be subject to him ... and a true wife accounts her subjection her honor and freedom..."³ Durable and static, the common law was reduced to treatise form by Sir William Blackstone, an Oxford professor. Blackstone delivered the common law to colonists in his four volumes entitled *Commentaries on the Laws of England.* After the Bible, *Commentaries* was probably the most popular book on the shelves of the English colonists. When the historian Mary Beard sought to emphasize the importance of equity law (the set of legal principles and remedies in chancery courts that supplemented strict rules of law operating too harshly) over the common law, she admitted the latter's primacy during the period. More copies of Blackstone's *Commentaries* were sold during the eighteenth century in America than in England, she concluded, and the volumes "were the standard textbook for the training of lawyers."⁴

Blackstone recognized the antiquity of legal practices that had medieval roots and that had emerged in a society where wealth was based on land. "We inherit an old Gothic castle, erected in the days of chivalry." Admiring its static propriety about family matters, he believed the common law was nevertheless "fitted for a modern inhabitant." For women this meant that "by marriage, the husband and wife are one in law; that is, the very being or legal existence of the woman is suspended during the marriage or at least is incorporated and consolidated into that of the husband under whose wing, protection and care, she performs every thing. … The Wife is under the protection and influence of the man."[5] And in the homely metaphors that Blackstone favored to enliven the often dry regulations informing the relations of husbands and wives, "Men and women are one person, but understand in what manner. When a small brooke or little river incorporates with the Rhodamus or Humber or the Thames, the poor rivulet looseth her name. It beareth no sway; it possessth nothing during coverture. A woman as soon as she is married is called couvert … clouded and overshadowed; she hath lost her streame."[6] The term "coverture," from the French verb for "to cover," referred to married women's legal invisibility. Husbands represented their wives in all legal, civic, and economic affairs, and thus a wife's autonomy and selfhood were non-existent.

Under such conventional wisdom and its resulting legalities, women could not vote, hold office, sign contracts, incur debts (beyond "necessaries"), sue, make a will, have access to their husband's personal estate, or control their own earnings. A woman's husband was the automatic legal guardian of her children. In one symbolic expression of domestic relations under the common law, the taking of a husband's life by a wife was considered treason and came with harsher penalties than those of ordinary murder. Some of these discriminations existed because married women could not own property in fee simple, that is, property that did not have restrictions on its disposal. Critically, since property was the measure of voting privileges and office holding for men in the eighteenth and early nineteenth centuries, married women could not vote. For example, in most states after the American Revolution either by statute or constitution, men were specifically named as voters, typically earning the privilege through their stake in society. Thus they had to pay forty shillings of taxes or else rent property worth an amount specified by the state government. And because women could not vote, they had neither authority nor political presence. Aptly the women at Seneca Falls described their condition, quoting Blackstone, as one of being "civilly dead."

Femes soles—that is women who never married or who were widows—had more privileges in the public world, at least insofar as economic arrangements were concerned. Colonial historians have made much of the better comparative circumstances of American women, especially femes soles, to those of British women. colonial women, married and unmarried, like Judith Murray of Massachusetts, Martha Ballard of Maine, and Mary Katherine Goddard and Margaret Brent of Maryland, moved beyond domesticity to earn money as midwives, run businesses and newspapers, trade and handle money, and in the latter's case, unsuccessfully petition the courts for the right to vote.[7] But most of the privileges of single women related to their ability to act as economic persons. For they, like their married sisters, could not vote, no matter how much property they owned.

There were other areas of female activity beyond the domestic, always notable for their exceptionalism rather than their typicality. Husbands did occasionally grant wives power of attorney over their estates, and married women did manage property, perhaps more so in the American colonies than in Great Britain, because of the periodic absences of men in a less settled society. Usually, however, these were for specific tasks and lengths of time. If a husband did not fulfill his obligation of leaving his wife a life interest in one-third of his real estate (but not his personal property), she could sue. In order that she did not become a public charge, courts generally ruled for the widow. Again these were exceptions to the general classification of adult women in the common law as legally and politically more like children, servants, and slaves than adult white males.

By the time of the American Revolution, the common law of domestic relations had been assimilated into the laws of each colony. Thus after the Revolution the doctrine of coverture remained in state law and survived in some cases into the twentieth century in a society that venerated the family as a basic mechanism of stability. Even as familial arrangements changed from those of extended-kinship landed units to those of smaller nuclear units, the doctrine of coverture still applied. The common law, as legal historian Reva Siegel has written, "understood the family as a domain of law and governance, a gendered jurisdiction … . The common law empowered the head of the household to govern its dependent members and to represent them to third parties."[8]

For centuries, the female's status as wife and mother in the common law remained the judicial undergirding of a political culture that denied women public rights of voting and sitting on juries, and the private right to be safe and secure in their households. Indeed, under the common law husbands held "the right of correction" over their wives. States continued to establish arbitrary gendered rules for such matters as jury duty with little intervention from Congress and the Supreme Court until the 1970s and 1980s. And only in those decades did the American judicial system begin to acknowledge the possibility of marital rape, a notion that turned on its head the common law notion that wives were the possessions of their husbands.

From 1776 to 1920 and beyond, American families were little commonwealths organized on the principle that the father and husband was the patriarch. In law, a married couple was a unit and he spoke and acted for that unit. There could be no democracy here, nor any notions of republicanism based on an understanding that women, like men, could serve the body politic. Increasingly, a whole arena of characteristics associated with the American Revolution separated men and women. Men claimed patriotism, courageous military service, and even participation in civic matters as those requirements for active membership in the republic. But women could not serve in the military (and more importantly in this generation, in the local militias), nor could they vote. Lacking autonomy by law and public opinion, women were stereotyped as frivolous and dependent. They lacked the essential ingredient of self-discipline required for manly citizens who must govern themselves as they governed their society. At most, as the historian Linda Kerber has explained, they could only serve as "republican mothers," teaching their sons the patriotic attributes needed for their public roles in the new United States of America.

Women owed duty and service to their husbands while their male family members owed them protection and economic support. This principle of the male breadwinner later undermined women's ability to gain fairness in the marketplace. Meanwhile the obligation of wives and daughters within this hierarchy was such that obligations to husbands and fathers took precedence over their loyalty to the state.[9] When women appeared at all in legal documents, it was as wife, daughter, sister, or widow of a free man to whom they legally belonged.[10]

The reverence for the common law on both sides of the Atlantic continued to place all women in a subordinate role. By extension from the typical, expected role for women as wives, the never-married and the widowed also had no civic presence. The femes soles paid taxes, but could not vote. And if they refused to pay their taxes because they were not represented in state legislatures and in Congress, their property was seized. In one famous case cited by suffragists, the eighty-year-old Smith sisters of Glastonbury, Connecticut, refused to pay their taxes in the 1870s and had their cows, evocatively named Taxey and Votey, taken away and sold to meet their obligation by the local tax collector.[11]

2

The Declaration of Independence

istorians still argue over the degree to which the American Revolution changed the status of women, blacks—slave and free—and the nonpropertied. There is certainly evidence that after the Revolution women gained more inheritance rights: their dower rights were more likely to come with outright ownership rather than a life-interest in their husband's property. There were more divorces initiated by women, though these were, in any case, extremely rare.[12] But the new states of the republic mostly continued traditional practices relating to the common law of domestic relationships.[13] In some states, the common law was specifically transported into written constitutions and statute law. Incontestably, what changed was the political leadership of the community, not civil rights for women.

At the beginning of the American Revolution, colonial leaders justified their extraordinary behavior in the text of the Declaration of Independence, written in 1776 principally by Thomas Jefferson. In the process of indicting George III for his "repeated injuries and usurpations," the Continental Congress proclaimed a commitment to natural law—a different species of law from common, equity, statute, and constitutional law—and one that would be used by women to argue for their rights.

Jefferson's words still resonate among the powerless, and have often been used to justify political upheavals in other nations: "We hold these truths to be self-evident: That all men are created equal, that they are endowed by their Creator with certain unalienable rights; that among these are life, liberty, and the pursuit of happiness and that, to secure these rights, governments are instituted among men, deriving their just powers from the consent of the governed." While the reference is to men, the universality of the principles, though not the language, acknowledged that all humans were part of the natural law and that potentially there might be a public space for women. According to the English philosopher John Locke, all men held certain rights in a state of nature. They retained some of these rights when they gave their allegiance to their governors. Clearly Lockean natural rights could be taken to imply gender equality, for it was not preposterous to think that all humans held these rights in that abstraction of "the state of nature."

Three-quarters of a century after the writing of the Declaration of Independence, the women of Seneca Falls used its claims of injustice under natural law to demand the end of coverture and the beginning of political equality for women as individuals no longer defined by their family status. There would be no violence in their revolution, only occasional acts of civil disobedience. Yet to override the common law of domesticity with natural law, and to establish women—even philosophically, much less legally—as autonomous persons would require a transformation in attitudes and values. And the definition of natural rights rested in the minds of men.

The American Revolution brought no immediate end to the common law of domestic relations that was the source of women's legal excision from the body politic. As Linda Kerber has written, the men of the Revolution "left intact the system of the old English law of domestic relations. This system of law was among the many elements of English common law that were quietly absorbed into American legal practice in order to save the trouble of restating what seemed obvious."[14] In Maryland, for example, the state's new constitution of 1776 declared that its inhabitants "were entitled to common law." Lowering the property requirements for male voting, Maryland's constitution in its Declaration of Rights masculinized the suffrage, requiring "every man having property, and a common interest with and attachment to the community, ought to have a right to suffrage." Yet in the section on the community's claims to taxes, the language changed to require contributions from every *person*.

Only New Jersey's hastily drawn 1776 constitution extended the franchise to "all inhabitants of the State of full age who are worth fifty pounds, ... [who have] clear estates to the same and have resided within the county in which they claim their Vote for twelve months." Under these arrangements, New Jersey women could and did vote. But as Joan Hoff has pointed out, even that state's liberal Quaker tradition could not withstand "the patriarchal and postrevolutionary republican attitudes about women for very long." In 1807, New Jersey women were disenfranchised by a law that went unchallenged and eventually won even greater legal support in the constitutional reforms of 1844. Meanwhile, the Supreme Court of the state offered an explanation that survived, in one form or another, into the twentieth century: "Female reserve and delicacy are incompatible with the duties of a free elector."[15]

During these revolutionary times, there were a few rhetorical objections that such a tyrannical system of domestic relations should not survive the new political experiment in "freedom and liberty" as the benchmarks of human governance. Applying the logic of the Declaration of Independence, Bostonian James Otis, a fervent supporter of the Revolution, wondered "if all were reduced to a state of nature, had not apple women and orange girls as good a right to give their respectable suffrages for a new king as the philosopher, courtier, and politician?"[16]

Meanwhile Abigail Adams, the year before the Declaration of Independence was written and well before the success of the revolutionaries, queried her husband John: "if we separate from Britain what code of laws will be established?" A year later, with John in Congress in Philadelphia, she famously advised him to remember the ladies and "be more generous and favorable to them than your ancestors." In sentences that spoke to the diminished position of women in the common law, she advised, "Do not put such unlimited power into the hands of the Husbands. Remember all Men would be tyrants if they could. If particular care and attention is not paid to the Ladies, we are determined to foment a rebellion and will not hold ourselves bound by laws in which we have no voice or representation." And a few weeks later, she repeated her earlier point: "… for whilst you are proclaiming peace and Good will to men, Emancipating all Nations, you insist upon retaining absolute power over Wives."[17] Rather than a plea to vote as it is often misrepresented, hers was a retrospective comment on the dependency of women under the common law.

Even so, during the Revolution, American women offered no protest on the level of the Frenchwoman Olympe de Gouges, who published a spirited response to the male-authored "Declaration of the Rights of Man and the Citizen." Written in 1791, Gouges' "Declaration of Woman and the Rights of the Citizen" demanded all the political rights of men, and proclaimed that "woman is born free and lives equal to man in her rights." There were at various times during the French Revolution organized women's societies that sought the vote. Sufficiently threatening, Gouges was eventually dispatched to the guillotine.[18]

3

The United States Constitution

*I*n 1787, fifty-five white men gathered in Philadelphia to write a new charter of government, adequate to "the exigencies of the government and the preservation of the Union," according to the call for a meeting written by Alexander Hamilton. The Articles of Confederation, the first attempt to create some form of national government, placed too much authority, it was thought, in the hands of the states. The union that it named as "perpetual" floundered amidst the prerogatives and jealousies of the thirteen former colonies. Moreover, the amending process required a seemingly impossible unanimity among the states.

Thus the intention of the majority at the convention was to shape a structure of government that would balance power within the national government among the legislative, executive, and judicial branches, and between the former colonies—now states—and the national government. Having suffered from what they considered a government that had trespassed on their rights as Englishmen, the authors of this constitution sought to create a government by the people who would choose its officers. In the minds of most of the convention's leaders, any new government must depend on the patriotism and virtue of the few, rather than the civic-mindedness of the many. The document that emerged from the secret meetings that took place during the summer of 1787 has been much praised for its durability, common sense, brevity, and flexibility.

Women had no part in these meetings or in the contested ratification process that began when the document was submitted to the thirteen states in September 1787. Only to the degree that the Constitution established a stable government and permitted amendments did the document affect the lives of women at all, for their governance remained in the home where men were their legal governors. Written in a political culture in which the common law was accepted convention—as pervasive and little considered as the air—the Constitution's omission of any congressional authority over domestic relations was natural. Indeed Article I, with its delineation of congressional powers

---

and prohibitions on states, left to the latter opportunities to continue the common law. Thus only by examining the intricacies of the Constitution do any possibilities for female inclusion emerge, though these would have to be developed over time before becoming obvious legal necessities in a society that proclaims its commitment to individual freedom and liberty.

The pronoun "he," a gendered pronoun in its meaning during this period of American history, appears thirty times in the Constitution. Adult males for this and many generations after represented the abstract legal human being. Hence the Constitution is both explicitly and implicitly gendered. Nor did the vaguer label "person" that defined the qualifications for president and congressmen (not citizen, not inhabitant, not even he, but person) refer to anyone but adult males. Yet this very vagueness led to an argument posited in the late nineteenth century that women were not specifically excluded from running for president, for they were surely persons.

On this basis, both the New York radical Victoria Woodhull in 1872 and the Washington attorney Belva Lockwood in 1884 and 1888 made the negative argument that, as persons under the constitutional requirements established in Article II, they were legal candidates, and could not be excluded from running for president despite the fact that they could not vote. As Lockwood acknowledged to reporters during her campaign, "I cannot vote, but I can be voted for."[19]

Only by inference could women be considered a part of the first words of the Constitution—"We the People." These words of the preamble clearly established the sovereignty of a populace that might be expanded in the future. But in fact the controversy in the Constitutional Convention of 1787 centered on the extension of nationalism in the preamble that omitted the identification of the people with their specific state. Some supporters of states' rights favored a simple identification and naming of states without including "We the People." In any case, conventional views of women permitted the authors of the U.S. Constitution to finesse any precise definitions of who "We the People" were or should be.

In Article I, women—along with three-fifths of slaves—were included in the numerical apportionment of 30,000 required for congressional representation and for determining direct taxes. Some historians have argued that it was radical to include women in any category on which representation was based. Such an expansion gestured toward moving from inclusion as a member of the body politic on which the delegation of powers was based, to the power to consent, that is voting and participation in civic affairs. If, as

Jan Lewis writes, representation was based on women, then the government served them and would have to attend their rights.[20] But such a position was distant from the minds of the framers and was never debated.[21]

Besides, children—included in the clause "the whole number of white and other free citizens and inhabitants of every age, sex, and condition" as the authors of the Constitution had established by June 1787—were included in the basis for national representation as well. A similar provision, the three-fifths of a slave compromise that gave the slaveholding South thirteen more representatives in the initial apportionment, hardly anticipated rights for slaves. A few states were more restrictive and based their representation for state offices in their constitutions solely on free adult males, but the main consideration of the authors of the Constitution was to have a national government while protecting states' rights. What the convention debated was whether each state should have one vote in the national assembly, as had been the case in the Articles of Confederation, or whether each state would have representation in Congress based on its population. The result was a famous compromise, but there was no consciousness or contemporary implication that the inclusion of women in apportionment represented a potential for change.[22] Nor was it used as one.

In the imprecise and brief Article III establishing the judiciary, the founders defined the jurisdiction of the federal courts. A few femes soles and even femes couverts emerged as claimants and plaintiffs under this part of the Constitution. For the most part, their cases involved actions against foreign citizens or governments, and until Belva Lockwood was admitted to the Supreme Court bar in 1879, women claimants were represented by male attorneys. As early as 1834, Myra Gaines Clark made a claim on her father's estate in a filing before the Supreme Court, and she would continue to do so throughout the century until in all fourteen filings were entered before the Supreme Court in her name.[23] Eventually the power of judicial review would be deployed by twentieth-century courts to overturn discriminatory state legislation, but in the nineteenth century, women remained nearly invisible in the law of the Constitution.

Some scholars have argued that the constitutional language of both Section 2 and Section 4 of Article IV afforded a significant potential avenue for the inclusion of women as citizens of the nation. Certainly these sections were used as such by women in the latter part of the nineteenth century. Section 2 reads, "the citizens of each State shall be entitled to all the privileges and immunities of citizens in the several states." Here, though never defined until the Fourteenth Amendment, the word citizen appears along with the bestowal of rights (privileges and immunities) protecting individuals from the state and nationalizing these entitlements. The idea of privileges and immunities was an ancient derivative of natural rights, appearing in England in the thirteenth century. Arguably, therefore, it represented no extension of rights for men, but its appearance in the Fifth and Fourteenth Amendments to the U.S. Constitution was important as a possible location of rights for women.

So too was Section 4 of Article IV, which guaranteed to every state in the Union "a republican form of government." Important during Reconstruction in the South, this clause was also useful for activists like Elizabeth Cady Stanton and Susan B. Anthony in their struggle for female enfranchisement. In 1878, testifying before the Committee on Privileges and Elections of the United States Senate, Stanton argued that the U.S. government was proceeding unconstitutionally because by denying women their public rights, they were violating the constitutional pledge of a republican government. In the promise of Article IV, Section 2, a government was not republican, argued Stanton, "in which the people are forever deprived of all participation in its affairs."

In their battle for civil rights, Stanton and other suffragists also used the prohibition in Article 1, Section 9 against bills of attainder (penalties that extended beyond the life of those charged or those affecting a group) in national and state governments. "A citizen disfranchised in a republic is a citizen attainted," she said. And, in her reading of the U.S. Constitution, the denial of titles of nobility in these same two articles against both state and federal government was also being violated: "When we place in the hands of one class of citizens the right to make, interpret, and execute the law for another class wholly unrepresented in the government, we have made an order of nobility. Universal manhood suffrage makes all men sovereign, all women slaves—the most odious form of aristocracy the world has yet seen."[24]

Such arguments were essentially anachronistic in terms of original intent. What was obvious to Stanton had nothing to do with the perspectives of the founders. The enlightened rationalists who wrote the Constitution entirely overlooked women who, unlike other dependent groups such as slaves and indentured servants, are not mentioned at all in the Constitution. As Joan Hoff writes, other dependent groups especially slaves are "euphemistically referred to and Native American Indians are specifically cited twice by name in the Constitution, but women are not mentioned at all."[25]

Their neglect in both the Constitution and in interpretations of the Bill of Rights confirmed the continuing authority of the common law. For example, the First Amendment granting freedom of religion and speech was not applicable to married women whose husbands controlled both. In theory, without an equal rights amendment, Congress, deferring to the common law, could make laws denying women's rights of expression. In reality, the traditional common law powers of men within the family trumped any claims for the private power of women and suggested the ineffectiveness of the First Amendment. When in the *Minor* case, Virginia Minor's attorney based his case for her right to vote on her First Amendment right of free expression, the court did not bother to respond to his point.

The Seventh Amendment's reference to jury trials and their procedures in the common law had nothing to do with women, who, while receiving trials by all male jurors, were often specifically excluded from juries by state law. As late as the 1970s, discriminatory arrangements for men and women relating to jury service at the state level still survived.

At the same time, the federal structure established in the Constitution, and especially the difficulty of amending the Constitution, often impeded women's efforts at reform, denying any possibility of national action in an age of states' rights. Defining suffrage requirements was understood to be a state prerogative, largely sealing off the possibility of federal intervention to remove "male" from the list of voting criteria. In the states, suffragists needed supermajorities as they faced complicated arrangements in state constitutions such as referendums and the convening of special constitutional conventions. The influential commentary on the Constitution, the *Federalist Papers,* reinforces this point: women were not mentioned, save in negative terms as in Alexander Hamilton's brief historical references to the frivolities of the Duchess of Marlborough and Madame Pompadour.

Ultimately the most useful article of the Constitution for equalizing rights was Article V, which established the possibility of change in the two-fold amending process. After the Civil War, the first article of the Fourteenth Amendment gave women a realistic claim, soon denied, that voting was a privilege and immunity of their citizenship. In time the amendment's privileges and immunities and due process clauses—the latter as applied not just to judicial procedures but to substantive issues—were applied by courts in the twentieth century to challenge sex discrimination. And it was through the amending process, in the ratification of the Nineteenth Amendment, that women finally became voters.

4

Constitutional Invisibility, 1791–1870

In the years after the establishment of a functioning government under the Constitution, the social, economic, and legal position of American women deteriorated. Natural rights theory dissipated, no longer appropriate to a fledgling government anxious for stability. Meanwhile, the doctrine of separate spheres for men and women emerged as the national ideal. Of course the concept of pious, chaste, submissive domestic women was not new, but becoming more popular in the spirit of these times, it reinforced the legal doctrines sustaining marital bondage. As women retreated into the home, and as the nation modernized and urbanized and more men worked for wages, the middle-class ideal for all women was to provide a well-tended sanctuary for their hard working husbands.

For women, private lives; for men, public roles—so went the ruling doctrine of this period. Given the conformity to principles widely conveyed by American culture and sustained by churches of every denomination, the basic charter of national government was often irrelevant to American women. Wives were confined in mental institutions when they ran away from abusive husbands or even when they opposed their husbands' religious views. Nor could they expect to employ the protections of habeas corpus writs. They had no standing in the courts to do so. An illustrative case can be found in Elizabeth Packard of Illinois, who was sent off to a mental institution because her husband despised her views on spiritualism. Packard had to wait four years, until her sons were eighteen, before they could use the writ to free her from the Jacksonville, Illinois, mental asylum in 1864.[26]

There were no women lawyers, and the republic's growing number of apprenticed male lawyers continued to learn the dictates of family law in the 500-page *The Law Student's First Book: Being Chiefly an Abridgment of Blackstone's Commentaries*. For decades Blackstone's *Commentaries* remained the basic text for training young lawyers, and so, according to Susan B. Anthony, the marital status of women remained "a regime of servitude for women."[27]

Men continued to represent women at the polls at the same time that household headship was used to expand voting privileges to previously disenfranchised men. State legislatures reduced the property requirements for male voting in the first decades of the nineteenth century, sometimes replacing them with a simple taxpaying criterion that many femes soles also fulfilled. And finally all such demands were relaxed, so that by 1828 only four states had any conditions for white men. Meanwhile, five New England states permitted black males to vote, and New York did so with a $250 property requirement and a longer residency requirement than that required of white males.

As for women and children, according to a Republican congressman in 1868, they possessed indirect, virtual representation. "By common consent or common submission whether founded upon reason and justice or not is not material to the argument, the adult males are supposed to represent the family and the government is not bound to look further than this common consent or submission," said Congressman John Broomall of Pennsylvania.[28] Household dependents did not have the requisite autonomy to enjoy the privileges of citizenship, and the marital unity established in the common law permitted one vote—the husband's.

Yet there were growing questions about this legal subordination of women. Some challenges were initiated by women in organized societies seeking to change public opinion. Others demonstrated the responses of state legislatures to issues relating to married women's ownership of property. Still other challenges were available in equity jurisprudence. As to the last of these, today the separation of equity and common law has disappeared, but in the nineteenth century, equity procedures were used in the special chancery courts established after the American Revolution by state constitutions. These courts were intended to rectify injustices through simple commonsense fairness.

The influential legal commentators of the postrevolutionary period—Joseph Story in his *Commentaries for Equity Jurisprudence*, published in 1836, and Chancellor Kent in his 1826 *Commentaries on American Law*—acknowledged equity law as a complementary system of law available for women in disputed cases of prenuptial contracts and the guardianship of children. For example, chancery courts sometimes assigned infant daughters to their mothers, thus controverting the automatic assignment of all minor children to their fathers that was established procedure in the common law. Married women clearly found some respite in equity law.

Yet Mary Beard, the foremost historian of the power of equity law for women during this period, has surely exaggerated its mitigating effects when she writes that "Equity had long been shooting holes in the list of married woman's disabilities ... ."[29] In fact, equity law was rarely applied, and Kent and Story's interpretations upheld the validity of the common law in domestic arrangements. Both jurists specifically affirmed the basic tenet that the wife's legal authority and existence disappeared after her wedding when it was dissolved into her husband's authority. The only free act of a woman's life, according to Kent, was the act of marriage.[30]

During this period state legislatures did begin to pass laws protecting women's property, which implicitly undermined the doctrine of coverture. These Married Women's Property Acts dealt variously with women's authority to make wills without their husbands' consent, to have estates freed from debts of husbands, to abandon the legal differences between feme sole and feme couvert in affairs relating to property, and to set up separate estates, though, throughout the nineteenth century, most denied women the right to sue their husbands. In Joan Hoff's careful analysis of these laws, by 1860 half of all northeastern and mid-Atlantic states had passed laws establishing separate estates for married women and had also abandoned the common law provisions separating femes soles and femes couverts. In the South, approximately a third of the states had done so, while in the West, less than 10 percent had established these legal displays of married women's independent legal existence.[31]

Sometimes, especially in the South, these protections represented the efforts of male fathers to protect the property of their grandchildren from feckless, dissolute sons-in-law. Intellectually these actions bore no relationship to any notions of modifying the position of feme couvert. There is some evidence that these efforts at relief for married women only codified what equity and chancery courts had already established on an ad hoc basis.

In New York, such legislative efforts began as early as 1836 when legislators discussed a proposal to change state law so that married women could hold title to property as if they were single. The same subject emerged in the state's constitutional convention in 1846 when, as historian Norma Basch writes, "The New York politicians squarely confronted the legal status of married women for the first time."[32] Bills to change the laws were debated in 1847, and in 1848 the governor signed the Married Women's Property Act, a limited modification that left unchanged the husbands control over his wife's earnings. Only in 1860 did the New York legislature permit women to control their wages. Of all similar state reforms throughout the United States, these earnings acts were the slowest and most difficult for women to attain.

In what the suffragist activist Elizabeth Cady Stanton later called her first speech, she laid out her claims for changes in the law to the New York legislature in 1854. These changes ranged from the enfranchisement of women to their inclusion in the legal process as jurors, to the need for women to have the authority to make contracts, and to control their property and earnings. "Yes, gentlemen, in republican America, in the nineteenth century, we, the daughters of the revolutionary heroes of '76, demand at your hands redress of our grievances—a revision of your state constitution—a new code of laws. ... Your laws relating to marriage—founded as they are on the old common law of England, a compound of barbarous usages, but partially modified by progressive civilization—are in open violation of our enlightened ideas of justice, and of the holiest feelings of our nature. ... The wife who inherits no property holds the same legal position that does the slave on the southern plantation. She can own nothing, sell nothing. She has no right even to the wages she earns; her person, her time, her services are the property of another."[33]

Women did contest the common law in the District of Columbia where the U.S. Congress held legislative authority. In 1869, influenced by members from states that had passed women's property laws, Congress passed legislation giving married women the right to hold property; to convey, devise, and bequeath that property; and to contract and sue. The relevance of such a congressional action was immediately seized upon by women who argued, unsuccessfully, that a federal Married Women's Property Act, by ending coverture for married women and giving them legal autonomy as independent persons, carried other entitlements at a national level.

Belva Lockwood, anxious to gain admission to the federal courts and to take on the contractual powers denied married women but essential for a lawyer, argued that congressional action taken in the Property Acts had in essence abolished the common law of coverture in the District of Columbia. But the judges of the District's Court of Claims saw otherwise. They dismissed such an interpretation, insisting that because the Married Women's Property Act did not explicitly grant women admission to the bar, it was irrelevant to Lockwood's petition. Later Lockwood herself participated in the writing of a bill "to relieve certain legal disabilities of women relating to their ability to practice law" in the District of Columbia. This bill, passed in 1879, became one of the first federal measures in support of women's rights. In these actions the importance of congressional legislation as a possible avenue for overturning the decisions of the courts denying women's rights was anticipated.

In the Northeast and in the District of Columbia, women used the passage of married women's property acts, whether they gave women control over their earnings or not, as ammunition in their battle against coverture. "It was the death blow of the old Blackstone code for married women in this country," concluded Elizabeth Cady Stanton in a far too optimistic assessment.[34] Instead the notion that the family was a form of government ruled by men and that the American Constitution applied only to white men (and grudgingly to a few black men who fulfilled its obligations of military service and who paid taxes) remained the main principle governing the relation of women to the U.S. Constitution until well into the twentieth century.

Some twenty years earlier, the specific philosophical challenge to the common law that spawned such activism had been developed at Seneca Falls, New York. In 1848, in a founding moment in the history of American feminism, five women applied the form and rhetoric of the Declaration of Independence to their challenge to men's social, political, religious, economic, sexual, and legal discriminations. Replacing references in the Declaration of Independence to George III with "man" and "he" as the source of their complaints, they resolved to end, among other changes, the legal discriminations that rendered them civilly dead and placed them in marital bondage. They wanted to serve on juries, to own property, and "to have a voice in the formation of laws."

Applying the laws of nature and the cue words of American representative democracy, they resolved that in a government that denied women the vote "all laws which place [women] in a position inferior to that of man are contrary to the great precept of nature and therefore of no force and authority." Such was Stanton's addition to the convictions of the founders: liberty was a natural condition for all humans; the Constitution's first phrase "We the People" included women; suffrage was inseparable from freedom; and taxation without representation was cause for rebellion. In its final form, only the structure of the Declaration of Sentiments was derivative. Of the thousand words in Cady Stanton's call for freedom, only 152 had appeared in Jefferson's declaration.[35]

In their own minds—and indeed in those of their contemporaries—the most radical of these reformers' demands was their claim for the vote. The women of Seneca Falls insisted upon "women's inalienable right to the elective franchise and immediate admission to all the rights and privileges which belong to them as citizens of the United States." But as Cady Stanton well knew from her own marriage, for men political equality would cut into their households, endangering traditional, comfortable domestic arrangements based on the common law. Men were the established, not easily displaced, sovereigns of the public domain, and most American women accepted male authority.

The Seneca Falls Convention and its Declaration of Sentiments spawned the women's convention movement of the 1850s. At first, this crusade for women's civil rights represented only a handful of mostly northeastern women, and its organization was fragmented, ineffective, and subject to ridicule. These reformers had expected as much. Meeting principally in northern cities, activists like Lucy Stone, Susan B. Anthony, and Elizabeth Cady Stanton began what became their life's work: "the speedy success of our cause depends on the zealous and untiring efforts of both men and women," they had proclaimed at Seneca Falls. At first, their movement represented no more than several hundred women and fewer men, among the latter Frederick Douglass, the former Maryland slave who had become a powerful voice for abolition. Most were veterans of the temperance and abolitionist societies of this reform period in American history. In those movements, activists had learned how to give speeches, to write pamphlets, and to organize meetings in the small towns of New England, New York, and Ohio.

Annual women's conventions—organized by Stanton, Anthony, and Stone—were a preferred method of staying in touch. At these conventions, women passed resolutions claiming their civil rights and more. Before the Civil War, their agenda was expansive, as they introduced issues that reached beyond changing laws about the vote and office holding. They especially considered matters relating to the family. For example, Stanton spoke to the need for liberalizing divorce procedures, changing the common law's automatic grant of child custody to fathers, and making marriage a civil contract in which property rights were shared by husbands and wives. The conventions also attacked the church as a complicit institutional agent in women's servitude and openly challenged the U.S. Constitution, which had, according to a resolution in 1860 at the Tenth National Woman's Rights

Convention in New York, "failed to produce or promote human happiness, and could not, in the nature of things, be of any force or authority; and it would be not only a right, but a duty to abolish it."[36]

During the Civil War, the female reformers replaced their campaigns for women's rights with efforts to emancipate four million American slaves. From the beginning, they urged Lincoln to free the slaves, believing him far too timid in his efforts. Anthony described his antislavery politics as "milk and water," and before 1863 she railed as well against his failure to accept black males as soldiers.

Still the discriminations against women were not entirely forgotten for the duration. At a meeting of the Women's Loyal National League—their organizational arm during the war—Susan B. Anthony and Ernestine Rose, a Polish-born suffragist, argued over gender strategy and the essentialism of sex in a prescient disagreement that mirrored constitutional issues in the twentieth century. "I ask you to forget that you are women and go forward … fearlessly, as independent human beings … . Forget conventionalisms, forget what the world will say, whether you are in your place or out of your place." To this Rose replied, "No. Woman should never forget herself that she is a woman. It is because she remembers that she is a woman that she is in duty bound to go for everything that is right, for everything that is just, for everything that is grand, noble, and consequently for human freedom."[37]

While the Civil War influenced the working lives of many American women and produced devastating family losses, it also inadvertently—for there was almost no comment on this at the time—included black women in the executive and congressional process of emancipation. Lincoln's Emancipation Proclamation contained geographic exclusions for freeing slaves. But it had none for women and was therefore gender-blind. Both black women and men were freed by the Emancipation Proclamation and by the subsequent Thirteenth Amendment, ratified in December 1865. Still, despite the previous negligent attitude of most slaveholders toward any official marriages of their slaves, the dominant notion of married women's coverture applied to black as well as white women. Black men were legal sovereigns in their homes, which led Frances Harper, the notable African American abolitionist, to argue that black women especially needed the vote.

5

Constitutional Possibilities: Efforts to Nationalize Women's Rights, 1866–1900

The post-Civil War period of Reconstruction afforded progressives an opportunity to include women in a national dialogue about freedom and liberty that, as it turned out, centered on black males. Aware of the possibilities during this congressional era of amendment writing—and especially for the potential of the Fourteenth Amendment's first section—women leaders of the newly created American Equal Rights Association argued that they had provided important service to the United States during the war as nurses, spies, and government workers. Coverture had not prevented their running farms and businesses. In logic similar to that propelling the dominant Republican party toward giving blacks more federal protection, veterans of the prewar women's conventions held that these contributions dispelled the earlier objections that women had no obligation to the state, only to their male protectors. "The constitutional door is open," wrote Elizabeth Cady Stanton, expectantly. "The time to bury the black man and the woman in the citizen" had arrived.[38]

Still the small cadre of reformers was rightly suspicious, because as Stanton observed, "the tyranny on a southern plantation was far more easily seen by white men at the north than the wrongs of the women of their households."[39] In time, these fears proved correct as Republican leaders turned their attention entirely to freed male slaves, denying the women's claims of comparability in their oppressed constitutional status. Meanwhile the Supreme Court narrowly interpreted the Reconstruction Amendments, delivering to states authority over voting and jury service.

While the Thirteenth Amendment abolished slavery nationally in December 1865, it proved insufficient in the face of efforts by white southerners to limit freedom by state-enforced black codes, vagrancy statutes, and sharecropping arrangements. By 1866, in the Civil Rights Act,

Congress approved the first statutory definition of American citizenship, with equality before the law as its central protection. No citizen could be deprived of the privilege to bring lawsuits, to make contracts, or to enjoy security of person and property. For the first time some civil rights—which earlier had largely been the legal provenance of the states—had become nationalized.[40] During the congressional debates, legislators discussed status differences between black males and females. Instead of creating protections for married women, however, lawmakers validated black male freedom by guaranteeing them the common law of wifely service.[41]

To establish a more powerful shield for black males, the Republican majority in Congress went beyond the Civil Rights Act to pass the Fourteenth Amendment, which was ratified by the states in 1868.

The first section of the Fourteenth Amendment granted citizen rights to all those born or naturalized in the United States, and clearly women were citizens under this wording. Soon afterward, in the Fifteenth Amendment, adopted in 1870, Congress extended specific protection to black males from state prohibitions against voting: "the right of citizens to vote shall not be denied or abridged on account of race, color, or previous condition of servitude." Many northern Republicans interpreted the passage of the Fifteenth Amendment as the end of the federal government's role in Reconstruction.

Leaders of the suffrage movement like Stanton, Stone, and Anthony were frustrated by their inability to persuade legislators to interpret citizenship broadly and to include sex in the Fifteenth Amendment. In a critical shift that displayed the nationalizing tendencies of this early period of Reconstruction, Congress now had the power of enforcement—at least on paper. But without the specific inclusion of women or at the very least favorable court interpretations, there was little to enforce. Lobbying for what they called "impartial and universal suffrage," women who had wanted to make common cause with freedmen now understood that their dream would be deferred; indeed, they feared that adding more men to the electorate would make their task more difficult, for black men would be "more despotic than even their Saxon rulers."[42]

The implacability and durability of sex bias based on traditional understandings of the family became clear during the debates over the Fourteenth Amendment. Friends from the past including Frederick Douglass and the famed abolitionist William Lloyd Garrison denied the urgency—even the suitability—of women's rights. It was, in the famous demotion of the female by Wendell Phillips, "the Negro's Hour. To include women would lose for the Negro more than it would gain for women." In response, Cady Stanton wondered if "the African race is composed entirely of males." But Frederick Douglass graphically argued that black men were hunted down, dragged from their homes, and hung upon lamp posts; only when women were lynched would they have an urgency to obtain rights "equal to our own."[43]

Nearly all congressional Republicans agreed with Douglass that black rights must take priority and that women's civil rights were so unthinkable that they must be postponed. In fact, Democratic opponents of black male voting used the omission of women as a race-baiting foil: how could Congress give rights to ignorant former male slaves and not their own wives, sisters, and mothers?

The more significant next phrases of the Fourteenth Amendment prohibited states from making laws that abridged the privileges and immunities of citizens; "nor shall any State deprive any person of life, liberty or property without due process of law; nor deny to any person within its jurisdiction the equal protection of the laws." While the Fifth Amendment contained similar protections for life, liberty, and property and due process of law, historically it had been applied as a protection from federal authority of individuals charged with a crime. It was also applied to residents of the District of Columbia. The Fourteenth Amendment would restrict states. Seemingly this new grant of citizenship under the Fourteenth Amendment immediately struck the word white from the constitutions of states that had earlier limited such standing on a racial basis. In the 1960s, applications of due process, equal protection under the law, and the "privileges and immunities" clause would become the means to constitutionalize women's rights and thereby address their civil disabilities.

In the nineteenth century, however, women found in the Fourteenth Amendment a barbed potential for nationalizing their freedom under the U.S. Constitution. Yes, they were explicitly citizens, but what rights came with citizenship? In congressional debate during the laborious process of writing the Fourteenth Amendment, several senators explicitly stated that while women might be citizens, children were citizens as well. And obviously anyone under twenty-one—male or female—should not vote. "The granting of civil rights does not carry with it political privileges," warned Illinois Senator Lyman Trumbull. "You wives and mothers and daughters ... are not to be considered as invested with the rights of citizenship," insisted John Bingham of Ohio.[44]

Under the common law married women—and by a process of leaching into a stereotype, all women no matter what their marital condition—were not fully adult and were still represented by their husbands. As the nineteenth-century social critic Horace Bushnell explained, "all women alike are made to be married whether in fact they are or not."[45] As the Supreme Court had decided about blacks in the 1857 *Dred Scott v. Sandford* decision, women also had no constitutional standing to bring actions against states for whatever privileges and immunities states provided to white males. In this period, the contested privileges were voting, office holding including serving as jurors and notary publics, and access to the professions.

In the second section of the amendment, which attracted the most congressional discussion, the word male, for the first time in American history, entered the Constitution. The section, which was never applied, dealt with the need to reduce congressional representation if former Confederate states prevented black males from voting. With blacks now raised to whole persons by the Thirteenth Amendment, the white, southern Democratic party stood to increase its representation in Congress by as many as twenty-five seats. Republicans needed to insure that blacks voted and that white Democrats did not gain these seats in Congress.

For women, the second section of the Fourteenth Amendment wreaked damage and humiliation because it made obvious that women were not to be included. After a century under the Constitution there had been no change in women's status. Now the U.S. Constitution had been explicitly masculinized; the potentially gender-neutral language of "persons" had disappeared. "If the word male be inserted in the United States constitution, it will take us a century to get it out again," predicted Stanton.[46] In protest, women activists lobbied senators, drew up petitions, and gave speeches. But erstwhile friends, and even progressive reformers like Senator Charles Sumner of Massachusetts, maintained that any inclusion of women's rights would retard the process of bestowing privileges and immunities on black males. In response, women activists turned to the courts.

The first case involving women's rights that reached the Supreme Court after the ratification of the Fourteenth Amendment came in *Bradwell v. Illinois*. Myra Bradwell, a well-known attorney in Chicago, had studied for the bar in her husband's office and had passed its requirements in 1869, only to be denied admission by the Illinois Supreme Court. That court had ruled that as a married woman under the marital common law of coverture, she had none of the autonomy of person and independence of judgment required of attorneys. For example, any contract she signed could be challenged given her necessary submission to her husband's legal dominion. Nonetheless she had, in the court's view, "ample qualifications."

Under the privileges and immunities clause of the Fourteenth Amendment, Bradwell sued the state of Illinois. By 1873, the case was before the Supreme Court as a challenge to sex classifications for married women, now arguably compromised by the privileges and immunities and equal protection clauses of the Fourteenth Amendment. As Bradwell's counsel argued, "The Fourteenth Amendment opened to every citizen of the United States, male or female, black or white, married or single, the honorable professions as well as servile employments of life; and no citizen can be excluded from any one of them. Intelligence, integrity, and honor are the only qualifications that can be prescribed … and all the privileges and immunities which I vindicate to a coloured citizen, I vindicate to our mothers, our sisters, and our daughters."[47] He made no mention of the equal protection clause that would later resonate in similar twentieth-century suits involving sex classifications. But he did make the claim that Bradwell's right of free speech and expression were being violated.

In his decision, Justice Miller ruled that the Fourteenth Amendment protected only the privileges and immunities of national citizenship. Becoming a lawyer did not rise to a federal level. Justice Bradley filed a separate concurring judgment that has earned a place in American history as a classic statement of the durability of coverture: "Man is or should be woman's protector and defender. The natural and proper timidity and delicacy which belongs to the female sex evidently unfits it for many of the occupations of civil life. The constitution of the family organization, which is founded in divine ordinance, as well as the nature of things, indicates the domestic sphere as that which properly belongs to the domain and functions of womanhood."

After a discussion of the function of women within the family and an irrelevant appeal to "the law of the Creator," Bradley concluded that "the paramount destiny and mission of woman are to fulfill the noble and benign offices of wife and mother."[48] In similar fashion to the *Dred Scott* decision, women had here been categorized as a special class of inferior citizen, who, according to the doctrine of separate spheres, existed in the home in their private roles, but who publicly had diminished capacities in their familial roles as daughters, sisters, wives, and mothers. And, as was often the case in their judicial considerations of women, the Supreme Court judges based their ruling on special insights about women that they had received from God.

There were other important judicial tests of the Reconstruction amendments as women turned to the courts and acts of civil disobedience. Women must "take our rights under the Constitution as it is, on the principle that all persons are citizens and all citizens are voters," advised Susan B. Anthony.[49] Led by Anthony in what was called "the New Departure," hundreds of women tried to vote in the presidential election of 1872. In some communities women were registered and then denied the right to vote when they appeared on election day to cast ballots. In others, officials refused to register them. In Anthony's case, after she had registered and been accepted as a legal voter in her local precinct in Rochester, New York, she and several other women handed their paper ballots to election officials who after checking their registration rolls accepted these ballots. Identifying voting privileges with citizenship, Anthony publicly invoked the 1870 Enforcement Act to both registration and election officials. The latter statute was intended by Congress to protect former male slaves' political rights in the South by granting access to the federal courts to those blacks denied voting rights. Now it offered women a similar protection. Women too, argued Anthony, could sue local election officials who interfered with their right to vote.

But the efforts by women did not go unnoticed by federal officials, who even jailed the local registration officials on the grounds that they had broken the law by registering Anthony. Meanwhile, the suffrage leader was arrested for violating Section 19 of the same federal legislation that was intended to protect black voting. Passed in 1870, the bill was entitled "An Act to enforce the right of citizens of the United States to vote in the several states of the Union."[50] Indicted, convicted of the felony of illegal voting, and subjected to a fine and six months' imprisonment, Anthony was prevented from appealing to the Supreme Court on procedural grounds. She was too prominent and well-known to permit such notoriety.

Throughout the case, procedural violations and interventions by federal officials were apparent. The case was presided over by Justice Ward Hunt, recently appointed to the U.S. Supreme Court and a recognized opponent of women's suffrage, rather than by a possibly sympathetic local federal district judge. Hunt refused to let Anthony testify, directed the all-male jury to a guilty verdict, denied a requested poll of the jury, and peremptorily rejected a defense motion to appeal. The court did not require Anthony to pay her fine and issued no bench warrant for her arrest. Hence she had no grounds for appeal. In the final moments of the trial after the guilty verdict, when she was permitted to speak, Anthony made her case on the basis that she was taxed and not represented. And she complained that she was not afforded a jury of her peers, for there were no women on her jury. The story of Anthony's trial quickly became a powerful piece of suffrage propaganda, though not a judicial landmark because there was no Supreme Court decision.[51]

In 1876, during the centennial celebration of American independence, Anthony delivered an address in Philadelphia entitled "Declaration of Rights of the Women of the United States." Hers was an updating of the Seneca Falls Declaration of Sentiments and her understanding of American justice gained from her trial, with the difference in tone obvious in a comparison of the title with that of Seneca Falls.

Anthony and her co-author Stanton called for the impeachment of officers who had violated the U.S. Constitution. Her eight specific articles of impeachment "against our rulers" listed constitutional abuses by federal officials and included the use of bills of attainder against women as a legal category, suspension of the writ of habeas corpus for married women, denial of trial by a jury of one's peers in the case of women (and indeed Anthony herself), taxation without representation, and, of course, the central concern—the denial of the vote. Her final article of impeachment condemned the judiciary of the nation that "has proved itself but the echo of the party in power by upholding and enforcing laws that are opposed to the spirit and letter of the Constitution." She pointed to "vacillating" interpretations of constitutional law as unsettling "our faith in judicial authority and undermining the liberties of the whole people." At the time there were other reasons not to give women the vote, but, as Anthony knew, the lack of any inclusion in the nation's original Constitution and Bill of Rights was one.[52]

In the same 1872 presidential election in which Anthony had voted, Virginia Minor had been denied the right to vote. Her suit against a registration official in Missouri worked its way through the state courts and was addressed by a unanimous Supreme Court in the 1875 decision of *Minor v. Happersett.* In refusing her a ballot, the local registrar Happersett had simply dismissed her with what he believed a sufficient explanation: she *was* a woman and *was not* a male citizen. At the time, Virginia Minor served as a leader of the Missouri Woman Suffrage Association and was a friend of Stanton's. Minor's lawyers—who included her husband—based their case on Section I of the Fourteenth Amendment. They argued that the citizenship and privileges and immunities clauses protected her right to vote, which had been violated by the state of Missouri.

Minor's legal counsel did not make their case on the eventually more fruitful grounds that the plaintiff had been denied equal protection of the laws. These latter grounds became the linchpin of the civil rights cases for women in the twentieth century, but in the nineteenth century, lawyers believed that the equal protection and due process clauses of the Fourteenth Amendment referred only to procedure. Attorneys of this post-Civil War generation, writes Leslie Goldstein, "viewed the equal protection and due process clauses as clauses about the way the laws should be applied rather than about the limits upon the content of the laws. Twentieth-century activists believed that the privileges and immunities clause was the really forceful mechanism that shields the basic civil rights of Americans from potentially oppressive state legislation."[53]

Minor's attorneys also included other constitutional grounds for their suit. They argued that female disenfranchisement constituted a collective bill of attainder applied unfairly to all members of a named group, thereby imposing guilt on the basis of who people were (that is women) rather than of any act they had committed. Moreover, preventing women's suffrage violated the free speech clause of the First Amendment and the Thirteenth Amendment clauses on involuntary servitude. To be denied the vote in a representative, constitutional democracy was a denial of free speech and tantamount to servitude. Such violations of civil rights compromised the freedom of Americans; hence the United States could make no claim that it was a republic as was promised in Article IV of the Constitution.

A unanimous Supreme Court had no difficulty holding that citizenship carried no necessary voting privileges. Having just narrowed the limits of national citizenship and restricted the application of the Fourteenth Amendment to racial considerations in the Slaughterhouse Cases, the Supreme Court, in an opinion written by Chief Justice Morrison Waite, held that "The [Fourteenth] Amendment did not add to the privileges and immunities of a citizen. It simply furnished an additional guarantee for the protection of such as *he* already had. No new voters were necessarily made by it" [author emphasis]. The United States had no voters of its own, and women had not been voters in Missouri or in the United States at the time of the creation of the Constitution, though they were persons. The justices ruled that "the Constitution of the United States does not confer the right of suffrage upon anyone and ... the Constitutions and laws of the several States which commit that important trust to men alone are not necessarily void."[54]

But as Joan Hoff makes clear in her analysis of the *Minor* decision, the court spent some time in its fourteen-page decision arguing that the United States was still a republic even if half its population was voteless. More importantly from the historical perspective of women's constitutional history, both *Minor v. Happersett* and the *Bradwell* case used parallel reasoning to the *Dred Scott* decision. Susan B. Anthony and Elizabeth Cady Stanton had long used the word slavery to define their legal status, and the court in *Minor* declared that women had no voting rights and were a special category of persons like slaves, whose inability to vote did not infringe upon their rights as Americans. Meanwhile, *Bradwell* continued the common law discriminations against married women. In fact, Justice Waite had Taney's decision (in *Dred Scott*) in front of him when he worked on his decision in *Minor*.[55]

Suffragists found further similarities between *Dred Scott* and the *Bradwell* and *Minor* decisions—namely, in their broad reach and in the expectations that these cases would resolve significant American conflicts (over slavery in the territories in the one case and over women's rights in the latter). Both the *Bradwell* and *Minor* decisions used extensive dicta and could only be overruled by a constitutional amendment. Yet both cases have largely been forgotten.

"One reason that *Minor* did not receive anywhere near the publicity and national attention that the *Dred Scott* decision had," writes Hoff, "is because it was not related to any important historic or constitutional events. It is well known only in contemporary feminist legal circles."[56] But if women were (and are) to enjoy a constitutional history essential for providing a context for contemporary judicial understandings, these cases are benchmarks in retelling that story. In substance, language and determination they suggest how impermeable the tenets of the common law discriminations against women as individuals were.

There were other judicial defeats in these efforts to enfranchise women by using the Reconstruction Amendments. Occurring at the state level and in the District of Columbia, they continued into the twentieth century. In one example, with former Congressman Albert Riddle as their attorney, a group of women led by Belva Lockwood and Sara Spencer, a local Washington activist, brought suit to overturn an ordinance that specifically conferred the right to vote on male citizens. Riddle employed natural rights arguments, as well as the first section of the Fourteenth Amendment as the basis of a case that as citizens women were entitled to vote. But Chief Justice Cartter of the Supreme Court of the District of Columbia dismissed the natural rights claim and suggested with evocative metaphors that "the constitutional capability of becoming a voter created by the amendment lies dormant as in the case of an infant."[57] Women, in the view of judges, attorneys, legislators, presidents, and senators, remained a special category of person who did not need the vote.

In another case, Lockwood, who had run for president in 1884 and 1888 in order to publicize the discrimination against women in their public capacities, sued to be admitted to the Virginia bar. Previously, after a long battle, she had been admitted to the District bar and had even argued a case before the U.S. Supreme Court in 1879. A charismatic figure and well-known lobbyist with powerful friends who were members of Congress, Lockwood had employed a number of strategies that moved her step by step toward her goal. After receiving a diploma from the National University Law School in Washington, she had successfully applied for admission to the District of Columbia bar, and then had written a bill introduced by Riddle "to relieve certain disabilities of woman and to prohibit their exclusion from practicing the law." Once passed by Congress, she used this statute to gain support for her right to practice before the U.S. Supreme Court.

But such authority failed in the state courts of nearby Maryland and Virginia where she especially wanted to practice. The Virginia Supreme Court of Appeals based its rejection on the common law disabilities of women. Maryland's highest court also rejected her claim, one of its appeal court judges praying that "the time would never come when the state of Maryland would admit women to the bar."[58] Petitioning the U.S. Supreme Court for review in 1894, Lockwood lost when, in *In Re Lockwood,* the Court held that the issue was controlled by the earlier *Bradwell* decision. When the Supreme Court declined to intervene, the Maryland decision stood as a severe limitation on the possibilities for attaining rights through the courts.

In fact, until the 1970s the Supreme Court rarely challenged state defined expressions of women's civic disabilities. There was no application of suspect classifications or heightened standards of reasonability, benchmarks often used in cases involving blacks. There was no sense that the state might have a compelling interest in its citizens' rights, a standard that increasingly influenced judges in civil rights cases affecting African Americans. Only in the 1971 case *Reed v. Reed* did the Supreme Court strike down a state statute on the ground that its use of gender "could not stand in the face of the Fourteenth Amendment's command that no state can deny equal protection of laws to any person within its jurisdiction."[59]

With access to the courts closed off, women activists of the nineteenth century understood that only a constitutional amendment could overturn their assigned status as citizens without voting privileges and as married women who could neither vote nor practice their professions. After their failure to be included in the Fifteenth Amendment, suffragists, through a legislative sponsor in the Judiciary Committee, introduced into Congress the Susan B. Anthony Amendment, which stated that the right to vote must not be denied on the basis of sex. Given the logic and justice of their cause, they believed that success was imminent, and so they optimistically numbered their amendment the Sixteenth. But for women, voting as a national right came so slowly that it followed three other additions to the U.S. Constitution: legalizing the income tax, initiating popular voting for U.S. senators, and installing prohibition. For years their Sixteenth Amendment languished in the Judiciary Committees of the House and Senate.

Republicans after the Civil War could calculate that extending suffrage to the former slaves would work in their political favor and cultivated the black male vote. Until 1916, and only marginally then, was there a similar partisan dynamic creating a core of supporters for female suffrage either in the electorate or within the halls of government. In 1916, Alice Paul, the leader of the National Woman's Party, tried to mobilize women voters in those states where they were enfranchised to support the Republican Charles Evans Hughes, who supported women's suffrage, rather than President Woodrow Wilson. But the effort failed and was considered an outrageous interference. Property-less males in the early nineteenth century and slaves in the 1860s had legislative advocates who supported the justice of their demands. Women, with only a few male supporters, were legislative outsiders with no leverage in their struggle.

Tabled or defeated in the Judiciary Committees of either the House or Senate until 1887, the Anthony Amendment continued to be voted down on the floor of the House and the Senate for thirty more years. There, opponents could count on the unflagging opposition of southern legislators. Still, the fact that the amendment reached the floor of Congress was a tacit recognition that suffrage was gaining support. Only in 1918 did it command the supermajority required for amendments, and then only after President Woodrow Wilson, himself a grudging supporter of women's suffrage, appeared before Congress to urge its acceptance.[60]

In the closing decades of the nineteenth century, women began to win the long struggle to change American public opinion. They used familiar methods. They created large national organizations such as the National Woman's Suffrage Association, led by Anthony and Stanton, and the American Woman's Suffrage Association (AWSA), led by Stone. Divided over whether to support the Fifteenth Amendment in 1869 because it did not include sex, these two suffrage societies represented two approaches to women's rights. Stone and her followers in the AWSA worked mostly at the state level and supported the Fifteenth Amendment, while Anthony and Stanton refused to support any amendment giving black males the right to vote unless women were included.

With the Anthony Amendment stalled and few Americans heeding their impassioned Declaration of Rights, suffragists traveled the nation, giving speeches, organizing and funding newspapers, writing pamphlets, and lobbying both state and national representatives. Narrowing their agenda, they focused almost entirely on suffrage, believing the vote the essential political instrument by which women could improve their status. When the courts insisted that the U.S. Constitution created no voters, the women cited the Fifteenth Amendment, which clearly was an instance of congressional enfranchisement. The precedent was clear: only when they could vote would they be an acknowledged part of the constitutionally promised "We the People."

Organizers hastened to any state, territory, or even municipality where there was a possibility of action. Given the federal nature of the government's structure and the tangled jurisdictions over voting—still so strikingly evident as late as 2000 in the case of *Bush v. Gore*—the suffragists faced endless campaigns to persuade state legislatures to take the word "male" out of their constitutions. Usually the procedures for any such change entailed a statewide referendum, followed by a constitutional convention or a supermajority vote in the legislature, followed by another referendum to accept the change. Without any electorate to place voting pressure on officials, women's issues continued to be dismissed. Before 1910, only Idaho, Utah, Colorado, and Wyoming gave women the right to vote in all elections, though some states and municipalities extended partial suffrage in local elections on liquor laws or on choosing the members of school boards.

In the immediate post-Civil War period, suffragists had lost referenda in Connecticut and more famously in Kansas in 1867, where a referendum on black voting failed as well, though not by as large a margin as that giving women the vote. Suffragists lost in South Dakota in 1890 and in New York in 1894. And so it went in a campaign at the state level that held few successes during the nineteenth century. What Stanton called "the aristocracy of sex" continued to deny the vote to half the population.

In the famous accounting by the twentieth-century leader of the merged National American Woman Suffrage Association (NAWSA), Carrie Catt, "To get the word 'male' out of the Constitution cost the women of the country fifty-two years of pauseless campaign ... they were forced to conduct fifty-six campaigns of referenda to male voters; 480 campaigns to get Legislatures to submit suffrage amendments to voters; 47 campaigns to get state constitutional conventions to write women suffrage into state constitutions and 19 campaigns with 19 successive Congresses."[61] This list did not include efforts to gain the endorsements in state and presidential conventions held by political parties during the period, though before 1916 only third parties—most notably the Prohibition and Socialist Labor organizations—favored "universal voting."

Opponents of women's suffrage—both male and female (Stanton called the latter "mummies of civilization")—argued that the state was an aggregation of families with males representing women and children. Female voting was unnecessary and dangerous because, writes Reva Siegel, "enfranchising women threatened the unity of the marriage relation, in which there could be only one will—that of the male head of household." Members of the Judiciary Committee of the U.S. Senate in 1884 used this argument of virtual representation and marital unity to suggest that "chaos" would ensue if man and wife disagreed: "the peace and contentment of the home would be exchanged for the bedlam of political debate and become the scene of base and demoralizing intrigue."[62] There were even threats that if women ever voted in opposition to the men in their home "unpleasant" consequences would sooner or later erupt. And turning this argument on its head, if the husband was brutal, arbitrary, or tyrannical, voting was no protection.[63]

6

Claiming Rights through the Nineteenth Amendment, 1900–1920

ven while their legislative and judicial efforts for the right to vote stalled, there were changes in women's lives. The symbols of this emancipation appeared in the high school and college diploma, the typewriter, the file cabinet, the sewing machine. More women worked outside the home in offices and clerical jobs and fewer, proportionally, in domestic jobs. By 1900, 60 percent of high school graduates were female and of the less than 3 percent of all Americans who attended college, 20 percent were women. A few professional schools accepted women, and by 1920, 1,700 women had completed law school and passed a state bar exam (as opposed to nearly 120,000 men).[64]

In one display of the power of the purse, Mary Garrett, heir to a Baltimore and Ohio Railroad fortune, gave money to a debt-saddled Johns Hopkins Medical School with the stipulation that one-tenth of each medical school class be female. Thousands of women joined women's clubs and particularly the Woman's Christian Temperance Union led by Frances Willard, who supported suffrage and encouraged her followers to do so as well. By 1916, Margaret Sanger had begun her public campaign for birth control rights for women, establishing a clinic in Brooklyn. Meanwhile NAWSA continued its efforts at the state level, and in the decade before the ratification of the Nineteenth Amendment nine other states enfranchised women, most in the West where charismatic state leaders rallied opinion for state suffrage.

While the claims were familiar, demographic arguments about the need for more women in the West, where sex ratios still overwhelmingly favored men, along with an arguably different attitude toward women in frontier societies were effective. Still, in the years before World War I, women lost referendums in Ohio, Wisconsin, Michigan, Massachusetts, Pennsylvania, and New Jersey. In the South, where the opposition was implacable on the issue of black women voting, they made little progress.

Judicial interpretations of both federal and state laws continued to single out women for special, unequal treatment. In *Muller v. Oregon* in 1908, the Supreme Court upheld a state law restricting the hours that women could work in a laundry. Previously, in *Lochner v. New York,* the Court had used the Fourteenth Amendment's due process clause to protect the individual worker's right to liberty of contract. Many progressives supported special state legislation limiting hours, night work, and overtime as a protection for women in a harsh industrial environment controlled by employers.

In *Muller,* the Court accepted sociological evidence that overwork might injure women as actual and potential mothers. The state owed them a special responsibility in order to "preserve the strength of the race." "History," wrote Justice Brewer for the Court, "discloses the fact that woman has always been dependent upon man. ... Differentiated by these matters from the other sex, she is properly placed in a class by herself."[65]

Others read the language of the decision as retrograde, given the Court's reasoning. In the words of the Court, woman "is properly placed in a class by herself ... . It is impossible to close one's eyes to the fact that she still looks to her brother and depends on him."[66] According to Alice Paul, such language incorporated the sentiments of coverture in the judicial clothing of the separate but equal doctrines of *Plessy v. Ferguson.*[67]

Alice Paul, a New Jersey-born Quaker, represented a new generation of suffragists. For her, in a judgment that proved correct over time, special protection for women in the marketplace was not an effort to protect a class; rather it reinforced women's inequality. Trained in the militant behaviors of the British Pankhurst family, Paul broke away from the National American Woman's Suffrage Association to focus entirely on a national suffrage amendment. Her National Woman's Party openly confronted an avoidant President Wilson who pleaded states' rights as the answer to women's suffrage.

But Paul and her followers attacked the president who controlled the Democratic majority in the House and Senate. Members of the National Woman's Party paraded in the streets of Washington, mobilized voters in 1916 to vote against Wilson's re-election in states where women could vote, and in 1917 began picketing the White House with signs reading "Mr. Wilson: You Promise to Make the World Safe for Democracy: Where is Democracy for Voteless American Women?" Arrested for acts of civil disobedience, denied the rights of political prisoners, treated as common criminals, threatened when they hunger struck with coercive institutionalization in St. Elizabeth's Mental Hospital, and eventually force fed, the women created an uproar.

Finally Wilson met with congressional leaders and urged support of the Nineteenth Amendment, which passed the House in 1918, but which required a presidential appearance in the Senate before that body capitulated. "If we reject measures like this, in ignorance or defiance of what a new age has brought forth," said Wilson, "they [other nations] will cease to believe in us."[68]

The ratification of the Nineteenth Amendment in June 1920 enfranchised women throughout the United States, and in the early 1920s it delivered significant change in the national agenda as personal, familial, and domestic issues became public concerns. A Woman's Bureau was established in the Department of Labor in 1920. The Sheppard-Towner Act, providing federal funds to establish programs in which public health nurses provided preventive health care to pregnant women and new mothers, passed in 1921. The Cable Act insured that women in the future would have a privilege long enjoyed by men: they would not lose their citizenship if they married a foreign national.

From the perspective of women and the U.S. Constitution, the Nineteenth Amendment finally ended the denial of women's participation in politics as national citizens. In so doing, it challenged central tenets about the traditional and proper role of women in public life. In a symbolic gesture that suggests just how deeply it trenched into customary arrangements, several lawyers, including William Marbury, a descendant of the justice of the peace of *Marbury v. Madison* fame, challenged the new amendment as unconstitutional. They argued that the federal constitutional amendment process could not be used to reconstitute the citizenry of the individual states, especially those who had not themselves individually consented to the change by voting to ratify the amendment. Therefore in a logical conundrum of Alice in Wonderland proportions, or originalism run amok: a change in the Constitution, agreed to by Congress and the states, could not legally become an amendment because it violated Article V that established the process of amending the Constitution! The U.S. Supreme Court in *Leser v. Garnett* (1922) would have nothing to do with such an argument, which would have undermined the Fifteenth Amendment as well.[69]

Although it seems clear that the Nineteenth Amendment guaranteed not only voting rights, but associated obligations and duties of political participation, many states initially prohibited women from running for office. The amendment, following that of the Fifteenth Amendment, reads "the right of citizens shall not be denied or abridged by the United States or by any state on account of sex"—a negative grant that in light of the African American precedent was intended to include other political activities. Yet many states prohibited women from serving on juries. The residual influence of the common law and the ineffectiveness of ordinary equal protection scrutiny under the Fourteenth Amendment still impeded women's efforts to end sex discrimination.

In 1948, in *Goesart v. Cleary,* the Supreme Court upheld a Michigan law that prohibited a woman from serving liquor as a bartender. In 1961, in *Hoyt v. Florida,* the Supreme Court allowed a Florida law to stand that did not require women, as opposed to men, to register to be part of a jury pool because they were "the center of home and family life." The expectable result was to produce a disproportionate number of male jurors.[70] Yet despite its invisibility in these actions, the Nineteenth Amendment did make a qualitative, though often unrecognized, change in the relation of women to the U.S. Constitution, because it provided precedent and legal justification for a possible new status of women as individuals with citizenship equal to men's.

Immediately after the ratification of the Nineteenth Amendment, Alice Paul, who had always believed that protective legislation violated the sameness under the law required for equal justice for women, began another campaign. She challenged Florence Kelley, the head of the National Consumer's League, arguing that special hours and wages legislation would restrict access to the job market. Convinced that protective legislation did not work to the benefit of women, in 1923 she presented to Congress her first version of the Equal Rights Amendment (ERA), which both the House and Senate buried for four decades.

For Paul, the term equality must entail equal treatment under the law—women's rights to "be determined on the basis of the same factors that apply to men."[71] In its first form it read, "Equality of Rights under the law shall not be denied by the United States or any state on account of sex." It was later revised to read "Equality of Rights under the law shall not be denied or abridged by the United States or any state on account of sex." In 1972, Congress passed this version of the Equal Rights Amendment, which likely would have guaranteed strict scrutiny of any legislation dealing with women as a judicial class. Eventually the ERA failed by one state of the three-quarters needed to be ratified. Thus the Nineteenth Amendment remains the only part of our national charter that specifically deals with women, and in judicial terms it plays little role in modern interpretations of the Constitution.

Epilogue

he Supreme Court continues to address questions of sex discrimination and women's citizenship under the Fourteenth, not the Nineteenth, Amendment. Such an approach shapes—and was shaped by—a tendency to compare problems of race discrimination to those of sex discrimination. Thus the judicial system did not develop an understanding of the radical ways in which the right to vote undermined traditional views of the common law and ended family organization theory in that women were no longer identified in an historic position of status inequality. Today legal analysis still omits and distorts the ways in which the Nineteenth Amendment revealed a particular species of sex discrimination different from that of racial discrimination in its history and contemporary meanings.

The way in which constitutional decisions are decided is a crucial part of our collective identity as a nation. Votes for women required an entire shifting of political understanding and a recognition that a qualitative change had been achieved. Historian Aileen Kraditor writes, "To endow the wife and mother with the franchise dissolved society into a heterogeneous mass of separate persons, whose individual rather than family interests would thenceforth receive political representation. For this reason the vote would not be merely a quantitative addition to all the other rights [such as guardian rights and ownership of one's wages] women had acquired in the preceding two generations."[72]

Contemporary areas of sex discrimination law, mirroring race discrimination, do not treat laws concerning the family as demanding any special scrutiny. Some legal scholars believe that by forgetting the history of the Nineteenth Amendment, Americans undermine women's meager constitutional history and overlook the ways in which the history of the struggle for votes for women shows that "equal citizenship for women includes freedom from subordination in or through the family." As Reva Siegel writes, "The debates over the Nineteenth Amendment thus memorialize the nation's decision to repudiate traditional concepts of the family that have shaped

---

women's status in public and private law and that are inconsistent with equal citizenship in a democratic polity. If concepts of sex discrimination were informed by the experience and deliberative choices of past generations of Americans, equal protection doctrine would better recognize forms of discrimination historically directed at women; and the law of federalism would take a more critical approach to claims that the family is a local institution, beyond the reach of the national government."[73]

Certainly while courts address overt sex discrimination, they do not react to seemingly neutral employment policies with a disparate effect on women, given their family circumstances. The great tragedy of the Nineteenth Amendment is that modern courts have lost the crucial context in which it was adopted. They have lost touch with its rejection of an outmoded ideology of family life that systematically subordinated women. And they have re-imagined gender equality as a limited doctrine divorced from such critical markers of male domination as the rape and spousal abuse targeted by the Violence against Women Act, a major piece of modern women's rights legislation that, in a mode reminiscent of *Bradwell* itself, the Court struck down as beyond federal power.

Suggested Readings

On the United States Constitution

There is a large and distinguished body of literature about the writing of the U.S. Constitution and its meanings. Most of this literature deals with issues of the tension between state and federal authority and the division of power within the jurisdictions of the executive, legislative, and judicial branches. Among the best sources on the principles motivating its authors is Forrest McDonald, *Novus Ordo Seclorum* (Lawrence: University Press of Kansas, 1985). Among the recent studies is a comprehensive effort by Akhil Reed Amar in his excellent and balanced interpretation of the meaning of the constitution in *America's Constitution: A Biography* (New York: Random House, 2005).

Primary sources include Max Farrand's useful multivolume, *The Records of the Federal Convention of 1787* (New Haven: Yale University Press, 1911), and the classic work of Alexander Hamilton et al., *The Federalist: A Commentary on the Constitution of the United States* (New York: Modern Library, 2000).

There are also recent studies of what is crucial in understanding women's relation to the Constitution. Among these are James Kettner, *The Development of American Citizenship* (Chapel Hill: University of North Carolina Press, 1978) and the essays in Paul Brest et al., in *Processes of Constitutional Decision Making: Cases and Materials* (New York: Aspen Law & Business, 2000). Jack Rakove's popular study of the assumptions of the founders lays out the ideological context for framing of the Constitution. See his *Original Meanings: Politics and Ideas in the Making of the Constitution* (New York: Alfred A. Knopf, 1996).

On the Common Law and Married Women Property Acts

William Blackstone's *Commentaries on the Laws of England* is the essential reading for understanding the common law of domestic relationships which established the status of feme sole and coverture. Robert Steinfeld's *The*

Invention of Free Labor: The Employment Relation in English and American Law and Culture, 1350–1870 (Chapel Hill: University of North Carolina Press, 2002) lays out the relation of the common law and its application to household relationships and governance, as does Hendrik Hartog, *Man and Wife in America: A History* (Cambridge: Harvard University Press, 2000). Nancy Cott's *Public Vows: A History of Marriage and the Nation* (Cambridge: Harvard University Press, 2000) makes clear that the institution of marriage, rather than being a private matter, has always been shaped by public laws. Morton Horwitz covers the post revolutionary statutes in *The Transformation of American Law, 1780–1860* (Cambridge: Harvard University Press, 1977). Norma Basch's *In the Eyes of the Law: Women, Marriage, and Property in Nineteenth Century New York* (Ithaca, N.Y.: Cornell University Press, 1982) discusses the early efforts to change laws of coverture that gave control of marital assets to the husband. Mary Beard in *Woman as a Force in History* (New York: Macmillan, 1946) argues that equity law was a moderating influence on the strictures of coverture. Also see Alice Kessler-Harris, *"In Pursuit of Equity": Women, Men and the Quest for Economic Citizenship in 20th-Century America* (New York: Oxford University Press, 2001).

Mary Beth Norton in *Founding Mothers and Fathers: Gendered Power and the Forming of American Society* (New York: Alfred A. Knopf, 1996) provides a context for the legal submission of women in the early national period. Also see David Kyvig, *Explicit and Authentic Acts: Amending the Constitution, 1776–1995* (Lawrence: University Press of Kansas, 1996) on the meaning of the various amendments. Jean Matthews discusses these issues in *Women's Struggle for Equality: The First Phase* (Chicago: Ivan R. Dee, 1997).

On Women and the Constitution

A rich body of literature in recent years discusses the relation of women to the Constitution. Of special significance in its coverage of the post-1960s era, contributed by both historians and legal scholars. Joan Hoff in *Law, Gender, and Injustice: A Legal History of U.S. Women* (New York: New York University Press, 1991) argues that the legal status of women in the United States remains based on male standards and that short of a feminist jurisprudence women will never be equal in what she describes as a legal dance of two steps forward and one step backward; that is, women get rights such as voting when they are no longer so important. Hoff has also collaborated with Albie Sachs in a comparative study of women's legal status in the United States and Great Britain in *Sexism and the Law: A*

Study of Male Beliefs and Legal Bias in Britain and the United States (New York: Free Press, 1978). Linda Kerber in *No Constitutional Right to Be Ladies* (New York: Hill and Wang, 1998) has used individual narratives to focus on the ambiguity of women's citizenship and the effect of the Constitution on various obligations expected of citizens—male and female. Editors Sibyl Schwarzenbach and Patricia Smith have collected a series of informative essays dealing with women's relationship to the Constitution from the founding period through the defeat of the ERA in *Women and the United States Constitution: History, Interpretation, and Practice* (New York: Columbia University Press, 2003). Sandra VanBurkleo's *"Belonging to the World": Women's Rights and American Constitutional Culture* (New York: Oxford University Press, 2001) is an excellent overview of the legal history of women from the colonial period to the twenty-first century.

Among the richest sources of information on women and the Constitution are law review articles. These include several innovative attempts to argue for the importance of reviving the Nineteenth Amendment, which does not play any role in modern constitutional interpretations and which properly understood would embrace a more expansive approach to issues involving the family. These articles are, among others, Reva Siegel, "She the People: The Nineteenth Amendment, Family, Sex Equality, Federalism, and the Family," *Harvard Law Review* 115 (February 2002): 947–1006; W. William Hodes, "Women and the Constitution: Some Legal History and a New Approach to the Nineteenth Amendment," *Rutgers Law Review* 26 (1970–71): 26–53; and the discussion of the Equal Rights Amendment in the *Harvard Civil Rights-Civil Liberties Law Review* 6 (March 1971). Also Akhil Reed Amar, "Women and the Constitution," *Harvard Journal of Law and Public Policy* 43 (1995): 465–80. There are as well excellent volumes that include the cases relevant to studying women's rights from the perspective of constitutional law. See Leslie Friedman Goldstein's *The Constitutional Rights of Women: Cases in Law and Social Change* (Madison: University of Wisconsin Press, 1988) and Mary Becker et al., *Feminist Jurisprudence: Taking Women Seriously* (St. Paul: West Group, 2006).

Alexander Keyssar, *The Right to Vote: The Contested History of Democracy in the United States* (New York: Basic Books, 2000) provides comprehensive coverage of suffrage. See also Rogers Smith, "One United People: Second Class Female Citizenship and the American Quest for Community," *Yale Journal of Law and the Humanities* 1 (1989): 282–95, which deals with visions of citizenship as they are expressed in American law.

The Suffrage Movement

Because the Nineteenth Amendment is the first and only mention of women in the Constitution, the suffrage movement is an important point of departure. The milestone in these interpretations is Eleanor Flexner, *Century of Struggle: The Woman's Movement in the United States* (New York: Atheneum, 1971). Aileen Kraditor in *The Ideas of the Woman Suffrage Movement, 1890–1920* (New York: W. W. Norton & Co., 1981) focuses on the changing arguments used by suffrage leaders as they moved from arguments dealing with natural law to those expedient reasons emphasizing the need to have women voters to reform a corrupt system.

Ellen DuBois has written extensively and informatively on the suffrage movement. See her *Feminism and Suffrage: The Emergence of an Independent Women's Movement in America, 1848–1869* (Ithaca, N.Y.: Cornell University Press, 1978) and *Harriet Stanton Blatch and the Winning of Woman Suffrage* (New Haven: Yale University Press, 1997) as well as her article "Taking the Law into Our Own Hands: *Bradwell, Minor,* and Suffrage Militance in the 1870s," in *Visible Women: New Essays on American Activism*, ed. Nancy Hewitt and Suzanne Lebsock (Urbana: University of Illinois Press, 1990), which discusses the importance of two Supreme Court cases in the history of the suffrage movement. Rebecca Mead, *How the Vote Was Won: Women Suffrage in the Western United States, 1868–1914* (New York: New York University Press, 2004) provides an explanation for the granting of suffrage in the western states and also discusses Paul's efforts to target women voters in the 1916 presidential election. These campaigns are also examined in Lee Ann Banaszak, *Why Movements Succeed or Fail: Opportunity, Culture, and the Struggle for Woman Suffrage* (Princeton: Princeton University Press, 2006); Holly J. McCammon, Karen E. Campbell, Ellen M. Granberg, and Christine Mowery, "How Movements Win: Gendered Opportunity Structures and U.S. Women's Suffrage Movements, 1866–1919," *American Sociological Review* 66 (2001). On the early New Jersey experience of allowing women the right to vote, see Judith Apter Klinghoffer and Lois Elkis, "'The Petticoat Electors': Women's Suffrage in New Jersey, 1776–1807," *Journal of the Early Republic* 12 (1992). Jean H. Baker's *Votes for Women: The Suffrage Struggle Revisited* (New York: Oxford University Press, 2003) is a collection of essays containing new views on the suffrage movement and its opposition. Also Jean Baker's *Sisters: The Lives of the Suffragists* (New York: Hill and Wang, 2003) covers five suffrage leaders—Stone, Anthony, Stanton, Willard, and Paul—with special emphasis on how their private lives affected their suffrage work.

There are as well extensive and useful primary sources. They include Ann Gordon's magnificent edition of the Elizabeth Cady Stanton and Susan B. Anthony papers entitled *The Selected Papers of Elizabeth Cady Stanton and Susan B. Anthony* (New Brunswick, N.J.: Rutgers University Press, 1997). Important as well are the volumes written by the suffragists themselves in Elizabeth Cady Stanton, Susan B. Anthony, Matilda Joslyn Gage, and Ida Husted Harper, *History of Woman Suffrage*, 6 vols. (1887–1922).

Notes

1. *Congressional Globe*, 39th Cong., 1st sess., 1866, 298.

2. Leslie Friedman Goldstein, *The Constitutional Rights of Women* (Madison: University of Wisconsin Press, 1988), 71.

3. Linda Kerber, *No Constitutional Right to Be Ladies: Woman and the Obligations of Citizenship* (New York: Hill and Wang, 1998), 9.

4. Mary Beard, *Woman as a Force in History* (New York: Macmillan, 1946), 78, 79.

5. William Blackstone, *Commentary on the Laws of England* (Philadelphia: Welsh Co., 1902) 1:442–45; 4:194, 203. For a summary of laws affecting women see Leo Kanowitz, *Women and the Law: An Unfinished Revolution* (Albuquerque: New Mexico University Press, 1967).

6. Blackstone, *Commentary*, 1:430; Christopher Tomlins and Bruce Mann, eds., *The Many Legalities of Early America* (Chapel Hill: University of North Carolina Press, 2001), 252.

7. Mary Beth Norton, *Liberty's Daughters: The Revolutionary Experience of American Women, 1750–1800* (Boston: Little Brown, 1980).

8. Reva Siegel, "She the People: The Nineteenth Amendment, Sex Equality, Federalism, and the Family," *Harvard Law Review* 115 (February 2002): 981.

9. Kerber, *No Constitutional Right*, xxiii, 15; Ellen DuBois and Lynn Dumeil, *Through Women's Eyes* (Boston: Bedford, 2003), 500–01.

10. Gordon Wood, *The Radicalism of the American Revolution* (New York: Knopf, 1992), 49. (In federal and state employment as late as the Depression of the 1930s under the one-breadwinner policy, married women were often fired, while husbands remained employed.)

11. Kerber, *No Constitutional Right*, 81–92.

12. Norma Basch, *Framing American Divorce* (Berkeley: University of California Press, 1999).

13. Lucy Salmon, *Women and the Law of Property in Early America* (Chapel Hill: University of North Carolina Press, 1989), 11, 17; Ronald Hoffman, ed., *Women in the Age of the American Revolution* (Charlottesville: University of Virginia Press, 1989).

14. Kerber, *No Constitutional Right*, 1.

15. Joan Hoff, *Law, Gender, and Injustice: A Legal History of U.S. Women* (New York: New York University Press, 1991), 91–103.

16. Bernard Bailyn, *Pamphlets of the American Revolution, 1750–1776* (Cambridge: Harvard University Press, 1965), 419–22.

17. L. H. Butterfield, ed., *The Adams Family Correspondence* (Cambridge: Harvard University Press, 1963), 1:329, 370, 402.

18. Lucy Moore, *Liberty: The Lives of Six Women in Revolutionary France* (New York: Harper Collins, 2007).

19. Jill Norgren, *Belva Lockwood: The Woman Who Would Be President* (New York: New York University Press, 2007), 133.

20. Jan Lewis, "The Representation of Women in the Constitution," in *Women and the U.S. Constitution*, ed. Sibyl Schwarzenbach and Patricia Smith (New York: Columbia University Press, 2003).

21. Max Farrand, ed., *The Records of the Federal Convention of 1797*, vol. 1 (New Haven: Yale University Press, 1911).

22. Farrand, ed., *The Records of the Federal Convention*, 1:444.

23. Norgren, *Belva Lockwood*, 199.

24. Ann Gordon, ed., *The Selected Papers of Elizabeth Cady Stanton and Susan B. Anthony* (New Brunswick, N.J.: Rutgers University Press, 1997), 3:345–50.

25. Hoff, *Law, Gender, and Injustice*, 117–18.

26. Barbara Sapinsley, *The Private War of Mrs. Packard* (New York: Paragon House Publishers. 1991).

27. Elizabeth Cady Stanton, Susan B. Anthony, and Mathilda Joslyn Gage, *History of Woman Suffrage* (Rochester, N.Y.: Charles Mann, 1889), 2:455–56.

28. Siegel, "She the People," 984.

29. Beard, *Woman as a Force*, 113.

30. Norma Basch, *In the Eyes of the Law: Women, Marriage and Property in Nineteenth Century New York* (Ithaca, N.Y.: Cornell University Press, 1982), 29–30, 64–66, 71–72.

31. Hoff, *Law, Gender, and Injustice*, 377–8.

32. Basch, *In the Eyes of the Law*, 150.

33. Gordon, ed., *Selected Papers*, 1:242–3.

34. Stanton et al., *History of Woman Suffrage*, 1:64.

35. Hoff, *Law, Gender, and Injustice*, 443, n45.

36. Gordon, ed., *Selected Papers*, 1:138–9.

37. Gordon, ed., *Selected Papers*, 1:492.

38. Stanton et al., *History of Woman Suffrage*, 2:174.

39. Gordon, ed., *Selected Papers*, 1:564; Stanton et al., *History of Woman Suffrage*, 2:317.

40. This is the argument of Robert Kaczorowski in his article, "To Begin the Nation Anew: Congress, Citizenship, and Civil Rights after the Civil War," *American Historical Review* 92 (February 1987): 47–67.

41. Nancy Cott, *Public Vows: A History of Marriage and the Nation* (Cambridge: Harvard University Press, 2000), 95.

42. Stanton et al., *History of Woman Suffrage*, 2:116.

43. Gordon, ed., *The Selected Papers*, 1:549; Stanton et al., *History of Woman Suffrage*, 2:382, 383.

44. Cott, *Public Vows*, 96.

45. Quoted in Siegel, "She the People," 987.

46. Stanton et al., *History of Woman Suffrage*, 1:569.

47. Goldstein, *Constitutional Rights*, 68.

48. Goldstein, *Constitutional Rights*, 70–71.

49. Jean H. Baker, *Sisters: The Lives of America's Suffragists* (New York: Hill and Wang, 2003), 85.

50. See *U.S. Statutes at Large* 16 (1870): 140–46.

51. Baker, *Sisters*, 85–6.

52. Gordon, ed., *Selected Papers*, 3:234–38.

53. Goldstein, *Constitutional Rights*, 67.

54. Goldstein, *Constitutional Rights*, 79.

55. William Hodes, "Women and the Constitution," *Rutgers Law Review* 26 (1970–71): 43.

56. Hoff, *Law, Gender, and Injustice*, 170–74.

57. Norgren, *Belva Lockwood*, 62.

58. Norgren, *Belva Lockwood*, 96–97

59. Norgren, *Belva Lockwood.*, 196–97; Hoff, *Law, Gender, and Injustice*, 184; Goldstein, *Constitutional Rights*, 112–13.

60. Baker, *Sisters*, 219–24.

61. Carrie Catt and Nettie Shuler, *Woman Suffrage and Politics* (New York: Scribners, 1923), 107.

62. Siegel, "She the People," 993–94.

63. The recent battles over the Supreme Court's decision in 2000 in *U.S. v. Morrison* suggest the limitations of the Fourteenth Amendment in establishing the national protection of women in their families and in rape cases. The Violence against Women Act had created a federal right in cases involving violence against women, but the Court declared the act unconstitutional because, among other reasons, Congress had supposedly exceeded the power given in the Fourteenth Amendment. The Court might have ruled differently had it understood the history of the Nineteenth Amendment and the struggle for the vote as a struggle against coverture and for the rights of women as individuals, thus challenging the continuing belief that sexual assaults and violence were private family matters. Critics of the Court's decision interpret the Nineteenth Amendment to upend traditional family organizational theory based on the common law and, together with the Fourteenth, federalizes women's rights to be free from such obsolete theories

of domestic power relations. See Peggy Cooper Davis, "Woman, Bondage and the Reconstructed Constitution," in *Women and the U.S. Constitution*, ed. Schwarzenbach and Smith, 63–67.

64. Virginia Drachman, *Sisters in Law: Woman Lawyers in Modern American History* (Cambridge: Harvard University Press, 1998), 253.

65. Goldstein, *Constitutional Rights*, 22.

66. *Muller v. Oregon*, 208 U.S. 412, 419, 422 (1908).

67. Remarks by Alice Paul, Convention of the National Woman's Party, February 16, 1922; Alice Paul to Helen Gardiner, December 20, 1922, National Woman's Party Papers.

68. Baker, *Sisters*, 214–25.

69. Siegel, "She the People," 1004–5.

70. *Hoyt v. Florida*, 368 U.S. 57 (1961; also in Goldstein, *Constitutional Rights*, 106–109); *Goessart v. Cleary*, 335 U.S. 464 (1948; also in Goldstein, *Constitutional Rights*, 102–103).

71. Noram Dorson and Susan Deller Ross, "The Necessity of a Constitutional Amendment," *Harvard Civil Rights-Civil Liberties Law Review* 6 (March 1971): 230.

72. Aileen Kraditor, *The Ideas of the Woman Suffrage Movement, 1890–1920* (New York: Norton, 1981), 25.

73. Siegel, "She the People," 948.